Salazar and His Work

# SALAZAR
## and His Work

*Essays on Political Philosophy*

MARCEL DE CORTE
PIERRE GAXOTTE
GUSTAVE THIBON

*Translation by* Brian Welter
*Foreword by* Marcos Pinho de Escobar

AROUCA
PRESS

Published in French as *Salazar et son œuvre*
by Éditions de Chiré (Chiré-en-Montreuil) in 2020.
Collected from the original essays written in 1956.
Used with kind permission.

© Arouca Press 2021
English Translation © Brian Welter
Foreword © Marcos Pinho de Escobar

ISBN: 978-1-989905-66-1

Arouca Press
PO Box 55003
Bridgeport PO
Waterloo, ON N2J3G0
Canada
www.aroucapress.com
Send inquiries to info@aroucapress.com

*From the French edition published by Éditions de Chiré (2020)*: The three present texts are excerpts from a work published in 1956 in Lisbon under the responsibility of the SNI (Secrétariat National de L'information). The SNI has chosen some European testimonies on the figure and work of Salazar. Great personalities need to stand back in space and time to be appreciated at their true value. But time has already allowed us to form a serene judgment on a work that now spans thirty years. And it would not be without interest to know what people think, in other latitudes and longitudes, of the figure of the great Portuguese statesman.

Only a few testimonies have been chosen which were thought to come from independent minds and to reflect opinions devoid of passion. For this present edition, we have chosen only the French texts.

# CONTENTS

TRANSLATOR'S PREFACE . . . . . . . . . . . xi

FOREWORD
*Marcos Pinho de Escobar* . . . . . . . . . . . . . . xv

Salazar's Work and Personality
*Marcel de Corte* . . . . . . . . . . . . . . . . . . . . 1

Reflections from the Margins of the
National Portuguese Revolution
*Pierre Gaxotte* . . . . . . . . . . . . . . . . . . . . . . 31

Salazar the Wise Man
*Gustave Thibon* . . . . . . . . . . . . . . . . . . . . . 41

ABOUT THE CONTRIBUTORS . . . . . . . 57

ABOUT THE TRANSLATOR . . . . . . . . . 59

# *Translator's Preface*

ANTÓNIO SALAZAR (1889–1970), Portugal's president from 1932 to 1968, was greatly esteemed by the three French essayists of this little book, Marcel de Corte, Pierre Gaxotte, and Gustave Thibon. Like Salazar himself, they come from a bygone era whose ideals may sometimes jar the contemporary reader for their simplicity and directness. And because all three writers saw many of their ideals realized in the Portuguese president, the three essays do not aim for objectivity. They present Salazar as a man who selflessly served his country as a principled and even philosophical leader.

Belgian classicist and historian Marcel de Corte (1905–1994) examines Salazar as both a man of his time and a man with a place in history and even political philosophy. His comparisons of the Portuguese leader with Plato and Richelieu reflect de Corte's ambitious and abstract ideas. Along with his very long and complex sentence structures, this makes translating de Corte, and Thibon to a lesser degree, challenging. Should the translator keep the style of the times in which these essays were written, the mid-1950s, or simplify such complex and meandering sentences?

If de Corte errs on the side of the big picture and the depiction of Salazar in almost idealistic terms, French historian and journalist Pierre Gaxotte (1895–1982) favors definitions and cause and effect reasoning. He discusses the meaning and use of politics, community, liberalism, political liberties, and continuities. Gaxotte's logic balances de Corte's sentiment. Naturally, the logic of definition and cause and effect are far clearer for the translator than emotion.

The essay from self-taught French philosopher Gustave Thibon (1903–2001) lands somewhere in the middle between the above two in terms of style and rhetoric as he reflects on Salazar's psychology. But this is not the psychologizing of psychoanalysts. Thibon's traditional understanding of human psychology, starting with the Christian depiction of the soul, leads him to evoke Plato and other lofty notions and images. This leads to a style and content that parallels the first essay. Thus at times, Thibon's ambitious and complex sentences are every bit as meandering and tough to translate as de Cortes'.

Overall, *Salazar and His Work* will feel outdated and pointless to most university-educated readers today because those university graduates have been educated to question and even reject their tradition and civilization while these three authors admire Salazar for faithfully serving his religion and country and as well as his tradition and civilization. These three essays are therefore not outdated and pointless, but highly relevant to the present cultural crisis in the West.

# *Foreword*

MARCOS PINHO DE ESCOBAR

A NTÓNIO DE OLIVEIRA SALAZAR was Portugal's Finance Minister from 1928 to 1932 and President of the Council of Ministers from 1932 to 1968.

A young and brilliant professor of Political Economy and Finance at the old University of Coimbra, Salazar was invited—*besought* would be a more appropriate description—as a last-ditch attempt to tackle the country's imminent financial bankruptcy.

Chronic deficits, excessive debt, a deficient tax system, among other domestic and international factors, had caused Portugal to literally run out of cash, both national and foreign currency. The combination of deep technical knowledge, solid convictions and strong character, enabled Salazar to embrace the daunting and vital task of stabilising and reforming Portugal's finances, preparing the path to the much-needed economic reconstruction.

The results were nothing less than spectacular. In just one year Salazar managed to organise the battered public accounts, turning the endemic budget deficit into a surplus — a healthy practice that became the norm for the following four decades. Foreign debt was paid-off, thus freeing Portugal from what Pope Pius XI called the International Imperialism of Money. Public domestic debt was sharply reduced, interest rates were driven down, gold reserves increased dramatically and the Portuguese *Escudo*, having appreciated and stabilised, was to become one of the strongest currencies in the world.

Nationally acclaimed as the country's financial saviour and admired for his intellect, work ethic and ascetic life, Salazar became the most prestigious person in the State — someone of Authority, in the classic sense of the Roman *Auctoritas*: socially acknowledged wisdom.

In 1932, with healthy public finances and a stabilised economy, the military who six years earlier had put an end to the severe instability and political violence of the Jacobin Republic, felt the need to institutionalise a new regime. Unanimous on what they rejected, namely a return to the permanent civil war climate of the party system and parliamentarian factions, the Army and the civil forces that supported them could not agree on or formulate a coherent and comprehensive political project.

Their obvious choice for the task was Salazar, who was appointed President of the Council of Ministers, i.e., Prime Minister.

Far from being just an economic and financial specialist, Salazar was also a political thinker who had reflected on the State and had a clear, well-defined architectonic view of a new regime, tailored to the specific conditions of the Portuguese society and the Portuguese nation, considered in the context of her historical origin and destiny.

Contrary to what many think, Salazar, as Prime Minister, did not hold absolute power. The power he exercised had been delegated by the military on account of his knowledge, accomplishments and unquestionable personal prestige. Actually, he had to mediate among the various forces within the power structure in order to guarantee the foundations he deemed absolutely essential, upon which to build the new political edifice. These undisputable "pillars" were, in Salazar's own words:

> To the souls torn by the doubt and negativism of the century, we try to restore the comfort of great certainties. We do not discuss God and virtue; we do not discuss the Fatherland and its History; we do not discuss authority and its prestige; we do not discuss the family and its moral; we do not discuss the glory of work and the duty to work.

Counter-revolutionary in its essence, traditional in its principles, Portugal's new regime — the

*Estado Novo* — rejected liberalism and socialism, as well as the totalitarian reaction to the weaknesses and failures of the modern State. Based on traditional Catholic social doctrine, particularly the papal encyclicals *Rerum Novarum* and *Quadragesimo Anno*, it had an organic corporatist conception of society and, whilst definitely being a regime of order and authority — a strong State —, it was subject to moral and legal constraints. As a "fourth position", scholars have categorised it as National-Catholicism.

It is not possible to understand Salazar without fully grasping the magnitude of the disorder and political violence that characterised the first Portuguese Republic (1910–1926), revolutionarily established and logical consequence of the imposition — *manu militari* — of liberalism in the XIX, with the introduction of the deleterious spirit of division into the national community, the abandonment of Portuguese tradition and the embracing of foreign models. In less than sixteen years the Masonic Republic recorded fifty-two cabinets, some of which only lasted a few days; of the nine Presidents of the period, one was murdered and only one finished his term; revolutionary attempts and terrorism were the norm, with the assassination of public figures carried out by groups such as the *Formiga Branca* (White Ant), the clandestine armed wing of the ruling Democratic Party, or the communist *Legião Vermelha* (Red Legion).

In his endeavour to restore four essential attributes to the exercising of political power — strength, independence, stability and prestige — Salazar condemned democracy, not only for its practical and observable results, but for its essential perversion: the obsessive notion that the number is the ultimate criterion of truth. Rejecting the "sacred" democratic trilogy popular sovereignty-universal suffrage-partitocracy, he maintained that the source of sovereignty is God, not the masses; that the universal suffrage does not take into account human natural inequalities; that the party system perverts national representation, working against the very principle of national unity in a logic of permanent "civil war".

As for Salazar's material achievements, it is not feasible to evaluate their true dimension ignoring the dire conditions at the starting point and the enormous internal and external hurdles he had to overcome. Suffice it to mention the stock market crash of 1929 and the ensuing world depression of the '30s; the Spanish Civil War and the massive communist threat; the World War and the new international system imposed by the demo-liberal and Marxist victors; the international campaign against European overseas territories; and in the '60s, the foreign-led terrorism and guerrilla warfare in Portugal's African provinces.

Despite all this, the *Estado Novo* managed to rebuild the country's essential economic infrastructures, such as roads, railways, ports, hydroelectric power plants, agricultural hydraulics, telephone network, etc. And carried out a vast programme of modernisation, industrialisation and economic development, through the creation or expansion of a series of sectors: electricity production, chemicals, petroleum, steel, metallurgy, cement, ship building and repair, agriculture and food products, textiles, automotive production, among others. Between 1926 and 1974 Portugal recorded the highest GDP growth rate in Western Europe. Its economy expanded at 6% to 7% *per annum* during the '60s and reached a growth rate of 11.2% in 1973.

Three attributes should be essential to anyone in public office: intelligence, integrity and dedication. If it is not an easy task to identify one of these qualities in a politician, much more difficult it would be to find two, and highly improbable to have all three simultaneously. For the good fortune of Portugal and the Portuguese, António de Oliveira Salazar was endowed—and liberally endowed—with this "golden triad" which defines the authentic governor of the *Polis*. Not only intelligence, but superior intelligence; not just integrity, but absolute integrity; not merely dedication, but total dedication to public affairs. In Salazar these three essential features were firmly anchored in a profound love of God and of Portugal. And this is precisely what explains the core of his political thought, in which the

Nation is the supreme value in the temporal order and the State is God's Ministry on earth to procure the common good — the legitimate material well-being, the development of a virtuous life, the salvation of the soul, concepts which are obviously unintelligible to today's materialistic, hedonistic and globalist frame of mind.

With superior intelligence, absolute integrity and total dedication, Salazar presided over a grand work of moral and material reconstruction — in this order, for he believed that spiritual values take precedence over material values.

He once said that those who should come after him would do different or contrary to what he did. His prediction was spot on. For five and a half years, his institutional successor, Prof. Marcello Caetano, did differently. Since the 1974 Revolution everything has been done in frontal opposition, the exact contrary, and Salazar's legacy has been dismantled, bit by bit, together with the nation — morally and physically.

In this book two philosophers and one historian take turns to explore particular aspects of Salazar's personality, political thought and work. With erudition, *finesse d'esprit* and superb writing, Marcel De Corte, Pierre Gaxotte and Gustave Thibon will give the reader an invaluable insight into the complex and fascinating nature of the Portuguese leader.

*Monte Estoril,*
May 2021

# Salazar's Work and Personality

MARCEL DE CORTE

TWENTY-FIVE YEARS AGO, DR. Antonio Oliveira Salazar left the small University of Coimbra and, against his wishes, was thrust into the leadership of the Portuguese state.

We must meditate on this anniversary.

To hold onto power for a quarter of a century without violence, trickery, or lunacy is a unique phenomenon in the history of the last few centuries, and singular in contemporary history. To have no other goal in those years than to re-establish the foundations of the Portuguese state, to clear out the debris that had accumulated from a long period of carelessness and anarchy, to reconstruct with a manly patience and inextinguishable faith, and to do this while ceaselessly sacrificing personal interest to the public interest without lapsing into a pretentious ideology is an even rarer phenomenon. To constantly have in front of one's eyes the principles that regulate the life of the city and, not deviating in any circumstance, to apply them with vigor and suppleness in the ensuing series of events and days that mark out the history of a people is unusual today. To blend vast and long-term perspectives that are not derived from a preconceived system with a sense of experience and possibility that does not fall into a sluggish and mundane political mold is actually unheard of.

It is, however, what Salazar accomplished.

We have to step back in history — way back — to find a figure to compare to Salazar. For my part, I see no one else besides Richelieu,[1] of whom Augustin Thierry[2] wrote:

> Everything that was possible in terms of social improvement in his time was carried out by this man whose intelligence understood everything, whose practical genius left out nothing, and who went from the overview to the details and from idea to action with a marvelous authority. He possessed universality and liberty of spirit to a unique degree.

Undoubtedly, the mission that the great Cardinal faced was easier and the slopes he had to climb less steep.

1   Armand Jean du Plessis (1585–1642) became cardinal in 1623 and was the chief minister to Louis XIII (1601–1643) from 1624 until his death.
2   Augustine Thierry (1795–1856) was a French historian whose works were permeated with the ideas of romanticism.

We discover in Salazar the same political genius as that which lived, perhaps against his own will, in France's greatest statesman. Like Richelieu, Salazar wants to serve the state, though he had no passion for it. Salazar knows what Richelieu did when the latter noted in his *Maximes*, "the great men who are placed in the state government are like those condemned to torture, with the sole difference being that the latter receive suffering for their fault and the former for their merit." As with Richelieu, "he loves more to be esteemed for doing good than for doing bad." Again, like Richelieu, he learned from experience that "whoever wanted to be considered according to the judgment of the common people often came to a loss, just like he who took the opposite view ordinarily found his salvation." When one reads the *Maximes*, one is struck by the analogies that move towards, until merging, the thought of Richelieu and the profound and perpetually overflowing intention that animated the thought of Salazar. It is so clear that, assuming politics is the art of application, underlying this art is an admirable science composed of a few obvious principles that, while inaccessible to the majority of people, govern life in society!

I've gleaned a few:

"Love is the most powerful motivation in the obligation to obey, and it is impossible for subjects not to love a prince if they know that reason guides all his actions."

"The state's reputation is preferable to all else; without reputation, all the men and all the gold in the world would serve us nothing, and our lives and goods would be exposed for foreigners to prey upon."

"Whoever foresees long in advance does nothing through haste because he thinks of it in good time, and it is difficult to do bad when he thinks about it beforehand."

"Just as different pilots do not place all their hands at the helm at the same time, so also it is necessary that only one take the helm of the state. He can receive the advice of others, and must even at times seek out advisors. However, it is up to him to examine the advice's soundness, and to turn his hand to one side or the other according to which he deems to be more suitable, in order to avoid the storm and keep on track."

"Up to two hundred of Samson's foxes agreed to burn the Philistines' wheat yet never did two agree to keep a chicken."

"The first condition of someone who has a part in governing the state is to give all of himself to the public, and not to think of himself."

"Everything exists only by the union of its parts in their natural order and place."

And above all this one, which needs to be engraved in golden letters in every corner of the terrestrial city and, if it were possible, to embed it in all the brains of the governed and governing: "In the things of government, the difficulty doesn't lie in knowing what is evil, but in finding a remedy that is less dangerous than the malady."

Whoever has not understood, after Richelieu and Salazar, that evil and disorder are inherent to man and multiply in every society because of his grandeur, that they are incurable as long as evil and disorder are not attached to a higher good and order, that we shouldn't force them by the remedies of quacks, charlatans, the enlightened, ideologues, or supposedly "logical" or "scientific" procedures, but that, on the contrary, it is important to patiently and tenaciously help nature to regain its equilibrium by raising it to the spirit of wisdom and unity, this person has not understood politics.

I nevertheless do not know why — even though the parallel may at first glance seem excessive — with Salazar I cannot help but think of Plato, but a Plato who is weighed down by the realism that great souls acquire from the effective exercise of power and that their wings remove in this world. Certainly, Salazar is not comparable to Plato, neither as a philosopher nor as a writer. Immense spiritual differences separate the one from the other. Salazar's prudent politics do not resemble the bold, dangerous, and often inhuman conception of the Platonic city.

And nevertheless! What brings together the descendent of an illustrious line of Athenian aristocrats with the humble son of Portuguese peasants is the elevation of their thought. Both of them, at the summits from where they descend, grasp political problems at their very sources. Those problems are made fertile and disciplined by the action of the statesman who irrigates the earth of man. Salazar's thought is undoubtedly governed more powerfully by an organizing empiricism that makes it narrower than Plato's. The dialectic of pure ideas dominates Plato's thought and leads him to arrive fearlessly at the amplest and vastest consequences.

But each of them wants to establish a state founded on justice, equilibrium, and the complementarity of its parts. Plato's failure only stems from the premature death of his friend Dion of Syracuse. A few remaining Platonic statelets thrived in Asia Minor. Finally, if Plato is a genius and if Salazar only wants to be a man among men, both are persuaded that the reform of the state is doomed to failure without the profound and radical reform of the souls of citizens and, even more, of those of the leaders.

Nobility of spirit, sense of state, ascesis and purity of soul: these three qualities are so rarely associated in politics that, without exaggerating things in the slightest, we need to go back to St. Louis and then Plato to locate the exact equivalent.

We can push the parallel further. And we need to do so, especially in an era like ours when human societies are tossed around—from incoherent multiplicity, which is a sign of sickness, to mechanical unity, which is a sign of death. The basic political problem is to know how to reconcile the living multiplicity of individuals, who are implacably separated from each other by their bodies, with the living unity of the city of which they are a part and which builds a type of communal soul. That seems easy enough in theory, and the human spirit has on paper skimmed through all the solutions to this problem! But in practice? We know too much, we "moderns," and by bitter experience, how most politicians who govern us wildly scoff at this crucial problem! Ceaselessly oscillating between the sedition of individuals against society, and that of society against individuals, they invoke the first in order to seize power and the second in order to conserve it. In the first phase, society breaks up under the pressure of factions. In the second, society is reconstituted in the most precarious manner based on deceptive rhetoric.

As how it has been practiced on the continent for almost two centuries, parliamentarism constitutes in this regard the most complete attempt at political blindness that the world has ever known. It sparked a reaction, under the form of totalitarianism, with the appearance of imaginary solutions that only continue through guile and violence. The history of our time ranges from the blindness of the confused spirit to the blindness of the illuminated spirit. Superficially, both the parliamentary and totalitarian systems seem in opposition, but at a deeper level they converge at an identical point. Both systems are the negation of the living individual and living society.

Pseudo-democracy and tyranny occupy the same line. Plato saw this better than anyone else. It is not an exaggeration to say that from the time of the decadence of the monarchical idea in Europe, Salazar is the only — or almost the only — statesman who saw this as sharply as Plato did. All of Salazar's written work is enlightened by the admirable intelligence of the ancient Greeks and Latins. This intelligence draws its strength from Plato even if it sometimes pushes away Plato's work like a vigorous infant pushes away his wet-nurse. Salazar's work stands against combined and contrary excesses. Like Plato, Salazar ran this risk in order to create a reasonable path against a ridge between two tempting chasms, in one of which the part devours the whole and in the other the whole devours the part.

To vanquish the multiplicity of irrational individuals who clash with each other and to avoid succumbing to the temptation to construct an artificial unity that compresses citizens instead of linking them through organic relations are almost superhuman feats. Salvation for peoples and individuals cannot be achieved if it is not pursued and brought to a good end. No one can set out to achieve this salvation without having a very high conception of the state.

A poor, debilitated, weak state, or a state in a condition of greasy degeneration, a state whose vampire-citizens drain its substance or an extravagant state that absorbs all the personal initiative are caricatures of the state. Whoever says state says stability, equilibrium, and balance. Whoever says state says helm.

It was the common destinies of Plato and Salazar to be born in eras during which the state was no longer a state. The most indispensable earthly function of humans for life and being fell into the rhythm of agitation or paralysis. Both Plato and Salazar felt the same terror and nausea when confronted with situations in which the state, either starving or crammed full, was deprived of its proper end, which is to establish the reign of good and virtue in the city. "The philosopher who is surrounded by the multitude that is ignorant of good or virtue resembles a man in the midst of ferocious animals," remarks Plato. Salazar undoubtedly saw it this way when he was elected to Parliament in 1921, where he sat just one day.

"Whosoever is a part of this small number of people who tasted the kindness and happiness of this good which is wisdom," writes Plato again, "when he realizes that the multitude is crazy, that there is therefore nothing healthy in the manner by which the affairs of state are administered and that he has no ally with whom he can come forward to help with justice without exposing himself to death, when he is sure of dying before rendering service to the state, when, I say, he reflects on all of that, he rests and focuses only on his own things, like a traveller surprised by a storm shelters behind a wall from the whirl-wind of dust and rain which is strengthened by the wind." That was Salazar behind the walls of the University of Coimbra in that crucial year in which Portugal, with no one at the helm, was in danger of collapsing. We have to reflect at length on the old Portuguese proverb that Plato would have found enchanting: "The boat which does not obey the helm obeys the reef."

The question that Plato and Salazar asked in these strangely identical circumstances is simple: "What does the state need to be in order to save man from drowning?" In spite of enormous dif-ferences in details, both came to the same con-clusion. The state is the helm of the social vessel on which the people of the same nation have embarked. A helm doesn't suppress storms or unfavorable winds. The sea and the sky are an inextricable jumble of good and bad things.

It is necessary as much as possible that the vessel engaged in this amalgamation avoid the bad and exploit the good in order to reach port. It is absolutely futile to believe that the long oce-anic journey of the ages will be paradisiacal. Who-ever promises us here below a pure good that is without a mixture of good and bad is a liar. Abso-lute Good is elsewhere. There is no worse misfor-tune for humans than to place happiness where it is not. In other words, for Plato as for Salazar, politics or the art to direct states must always be weighed down by a certain pessimism because that is what reality demands. The blind optimism of liberals and architects of clouds is a harmful absurdity that makes the statesman and, above him, the entire personnel of a ship, inattentive to the foreseeable menace of evils that are always keeping watch over the human race. Accordingly, it is impossible to promise to humans anything other than a relative good. Whether or not we desire it, the earthly good, regardless of its level of greatness, is accompanied with the shadow of evil. The statesman can never eliminate this fringe, no more than the navigator can evade the mutiny of the waves. The basic thing for the pilot is to use the helm to overcome the swell.

A good helm — firm, solid, well-built, and resistant — is therefore necessary. And above all, a man who is experienced at the helm, a single responsible man who watches day and night, his watch fixed on sky and sea, on the nautical chart, on the crew's work. You could make the best helm ever, yet without a good navigator, this helm is nothing. The state is inseparable from the head of state or the director commissioned by him to direct the vessel. And from that at least, good can vanquish evil to the greatest extent possible. While the vessel cannot avoid shifts in the wind or the favor or disfavor of the ocean in which it sails, it is still possible to avoid the change in pilot which is the root of incoherence and irrationalism. This minimizes error in direction. Humans cannot always flee the disorder that is inherent in the physical world, but we can always triumph over human disorder. A superior optimism is permitted and required for this.

But that is still not enough. The helm is not handed over to the arbitrary decisions of the helmsman. The state must follow the precise rules that originate from the reality where it sails and from the reality where the state holds forth with all its swelling sails. There exist laws of human navigation that are derived from the nature of things and of humans. These are the principles of the *lex naturae* that humanity has always recognized, even when violating them, until the day when humanity transformed the law into human convention. This convention is freely revocable according to majority vote in the manner of the sophists whose harmful influence, denounced by Plato, continues under our eyes. Just like the Platonic city, the Portuguese state founded by Salazar is centered on national interest, which is at the summit of the political hierarchy. There is no other reality on which the state can rest.

If the state must be stable, if it must be shielded from the changing passions and precarious wills of humans, it can lean only on the nation itself. Humans do not choose this nation. It is given to them at their birth. It is a common good that is woven from living relations that are prior to the individual, classes, daily matters, and everyone who is born, grows, diminishes, and dies. It is prior to the rhythm of generation and corruption, and is an earthly good though also "divine." According to Plato, this good, which imitates the eternal Good by its continuity, is the only venue where we can establish the state. It is also the only one where individuals can live on Earth. The nation that is abolished or simply weakened leaves individuals in a desert where they tangle with, collide, and hurt each other like grains of sand. Only ideological storms that incite these individuals against neighboring cities with a seemingly perfect unanimity can give them a common soul. In spite of all the international declamations, national interest, which guarantees internal order, also guarantees exterior order and peace. The nation is therefore the place of convergence for the state, the individual, and universal equilibrium.

Submitted to the national interest of which it is the flower, the state submits itself equally to moral and legal limits. Again like Plato, Salazar keenly saw that justice, with its foundation in God, surpasses everything that exists in this world. No flower can give its fruit or the seeds that perpetuate it without the sun of justice. This is not an abstract, conceptual, and general "justice." It is a concrete, incarnate, and lived one that recognizes the existence of natural or semi-natural groupings and the Church in the nation's interior. At the exterior, it recognizes the existence of similar national communities. Taken in its profoundest and almost Platonic sense, justice is nothing but the recognition of what is: everything that is — people, families, professions, local networks, religious beliefs, propriety, work, other nations — is sacred and must be respected. All of Salazar's speeches, like Plato's dialogues and Aristotle's prodigious metaphysical analyses, are filled with this sense of being.

But these speeches are discourses. "It is at the foot of the wall that we appreciate the mason," goes a proverb. Two centuries of erosion and destruction have destroyed the sense of the city, the sense of the state, and the sense of justice in souls, in intellects, in hearts, and even in morals. The rhetors' hollow declamations float in the blowing winds of the ruins. Where people deny that they are reasonable animals, only language is left. Everything needs to be reconstructed, restarted from the basic work. Words that have been corrupted by the sophists need to be straightened out, the reality behind each word put back, and each stone protected against itself and the entrepreneurs of demolition.

The temptation that attacks each statesman who holds authority is to do things quickly, to undertake massive transformations, to remake an artificial ordering of things, or, on the contrary, to maintain and conserve things "in place" by simply holding back the forces of destruction. Now, order is in no way artificial. It is natural and subservient to the rhythm of nature's growth. Order does not originate from only opposing disorder. In politics, nature does not create anything without intervention or the industrious aid of the person who marries and prolongs his momentum. A politics in the "fascist" style or a "conservative" politics would have been for Portugal a remedy as pernicious as evil, the first because it substitutes an ersatz for nature and the second because it contents itself with protecting a nature that is sick and ruined against infections from the exterior while the decay has already overtaken its essential organs.

What was and is still doubtlessly needed in Portugal — one can say the same about all the other countries of the world — is to combine in fair measure the respect of the tempo peculiar to nature and the active competition of the saving intelligence of man. This concordance is even more required because all political action, as Salazar wrote, is always limited. Now nothing communicates or inoculates hubris more than power. Power has a type of internal dialectical contradiction that cannot be tamed except by the energy and intelligence of whoever exercises it. On the one hand, power, as power, is unlimited. Taken alone, in its dynamism, it occupies all of the available space like a gas. On the other hand, it meets a natural, limiting resistance in its application to humans and things. The point of fusion and equilibrium between power and the reality where it operates is terribly ambiguous. The individual who possesses power possesses at the same time the sense of the real so that his action attains the limit at which it proves effective: Neither above nor below that point, according to the rule. And this limit ceaselessly varies, like the Platonic dyad of the Great and the Small, according to its place of application.

Salazar clearly appears to have this genius — there is no other word — of measure and limit that the Greeks, from Homer to the most celebrated of their philosophers, cherished as the highest human virtue. There is no doubt that his peasant roots powerfully aided him in his measured action. Only the peasant, submissive to the rhythm of the seasons and the sky and obedient to nature's injunctions, is capable of measure. That is why peasant civilizations were and remain the most durable. Only the peasant knows — not only by his intelligence and faculties of observation, but by being linked to nature with his whole soul and vital being — that the obedience to natural laws that limit his action is the indispensable condition of his personal survival and the success of his work. "You cannot make leaves grow by pulling on them," my friend [Gustave] Thibon loves to repeat. Slowness is the diligent companion of the natural end in the human order, which is also the political order.

A human is not an ephemeral insect. The life of a people passes from one generation to the next. Evil is prompt; goodness is slow.

To reproach Salazar for not healing his country in one stroke and not yet attaining, after twenty-five years of power, a total reform of the situation in Portugal, is a nameless insanity that testifies not only to a perfect ignorance of the depth of the evil, but to a perfect infatuation concerning the pertinence of the remedy. Let's listen once again to Richelieu: "It is foresight to undertake only what one can do and to put each thing in its time. Whoever does things like this is able to see most of his intentions come to fruition, and whoever does things in another way, in hastening his projects, shows more heart and ambition than wisdom and self-possession."

The hastening of history, of which Daniel Halévy[3] has so aptly spoken, is undoubtedly our era's defining characteristic. It permeates the immense majority of hurried and superficial spirits who are inclined towards the immediate. "Right away! Right away! Immediately! Now!," they all say into people's greedy ears. We are fascinated by the swiftness of the means of communication, the extraordinary dynamism of the modern economy, the spectacle of the collapse

---

3   Daniel Halévy (1872–1962) was a French historian whose defining historical work was *Essai sur l'accélération de l'histoire* (Essay on the Acceleration of History) published in 1948.

of empires, and the castles of cards built by the majority of revolutions. Yet the political, social, or economic order offers no quick healing. Nothing is built immediately for the good and simple reason, which is blinding to our owl's eyes, that it is a matter of rebuilding the mediating ground, the intermediate, the metaxa, as Plato said: the hearth, craft, and city which individualism and statism have devastated.

The living, organic connections, which are the intermediate bodies in a nation, take a long time to be rebuilt because they are cryptic, invisible, and infinitesimal. It is but an indicative spark, hidden in the depths of the human soul and still subsisting here and there, somehow or other. The lucid statesman, who knows that salvation is there and nowhere else, has to work on the infinitely tiny with an incredible patience and attention, concerned to avoid snuffing out this fragile flame. The gigantic and disproportionate means at his disposal are almost always inadequate for his true object. It is like shaping the head of a pin with a power hammer!

With a marvelous spirit of sharpness, Salazar refused to follow the path of Stalin, Hitler, or Roosevelt who did not cease to engage themselves in the easy work of forming immense masses where a human is nothing but a robot! At the end of the day, these maneuvers of totalitarian and pseudo-democratic propaganda only serve to hoist the puppeteer up on a pedestal! Life alone, true life, matters to Salazar, a laborer's son. Salazar chose and followed a path that stimulated fragile yet still-existing life, surrounded it with a protective framework, and worked obscurely, slowly, and obstinately on the connection of the human soul with the bodies of little intermediate communities in a way that once again triggered the circulation of the lethargic ancient energy. As he went, step by step, little by little, unemotionally and seriously, he was as peaceful and assured of the result of his efforts as the peasant who places into the ground the seeds whose invisible growth generates no noise.

After more than thirty years of observation as a philosopher of contemporary politics, I am persuaded that humanity's salvation rests on the undertaking that Salazar is attempting. Only in this way will we escape the collective death that is called socialism.

In an era such as ours, in which humans have lost the sense and life of moderation, Salazar appears as a type of genius. I mean to say that the Portuguese consider him as such, and as enigmatic. And from the faraway country where I reflect on his work, I am strongly tempted to share this impression. There is something profoundly mysterious in Salazar, in this statesman who speaks little and of whom little is spoken. That is undoubtedly an excellent sign of health, equilibrium, and life. Do not get others to speak of you! If statesmen were like that today, everything would be for the better in the best of worlds. Sparing in words is essential for authentic and profound life. Everything that germinates, ripens, and achieves perfection that comes from Salazar is filled with silence. The plant, the baby, the piece of art, and God's grace all develop with discretion. The authentic life is decidedly silent. Those who spark catastrophes, crises, disorders, fevers, sicknesses, revolutions, and death have one voice and echo.

But this silence accentuates the mystery. And Salazar is not prepared to break it. However, a few spoken words from two years ago in Porto permit us a glimpse of this statesman who is otherwise so sparing with information about himself: "I'm an independent man. I've never flattered people or the masses, before whom so many bend their knees in an attitude of hypocritical or abject servility. I am, as far as possible, a free man... I have tried hard to better understand people and life. I was human."

The whole secret of Salazar, it seems to me, is condensed in this undoubtedly unique testimony that he gives of himself. It is enough to extract the honey of these noble words to penetrate them and understand how Salazar arises, like a genius of moderation, in our world which is in the grip of immoderation and the inescapable chastisement that outraged reality inflicts on it. Greek tragedy in its entirety is relocated in our day in the history of the nations.

What Salazar gives us here is not only the fundamental character of his personality, but above all the essential aspects of power that he handles as how this is understood and accepted by the people.

Above all, power must be independent. If it is dependent, it is not a power, but the exact opposite of power. It is essential to power to be independent of every other person except the one who assumes it. As Bonald[4] wrote magnificently, power is a seamless garment that is not shared. The majority of people today misunderstand this evidence, although the battles that rage among them for the possession of power vividly accentuate this evidence. But if power only depends on one individual — in the family, in the company, in the nation — it is submitted to the good which is fitting for the end towards which it moves: to the family, to commerce, to the nations themselves. The power that measures everything is itself measured by the Good that everything contains. Transcendent to people, it is transcended by the Good that it pursues. Now, the Good is not what it is unless it is first known: *nihil volitum nisi precognitum*. "I tried hard, "said Salazar, "to better understand men and life." Ultimately, it is intelligence that communicates moderation to power and to the independent man who possesses it.

---

4   Louis de Bonald (1754–1840) was a French counter-revolutionary philosopher and politician.

The understanding of the Good is the only path that power can follow in order to escape immoderation and the demon of the ego that lies in wait to monopolize power. What is peculiar to intelligence is that it completely erases itself in front of its object. When a child discovers by its intelligence that two plus two equal four, it accesses a domain where the claws of its ego have not the slightest effect. It is by his sharp intelligence of the national well-being that Salazar constantly masters the power that he possesses but that degenerates with others into a vain exaltation of the ego. At the limit of this dialectic of moderation, it is no longer Salazar who exercises the power which he holds. Rather, Portugal becomes in some way transparent to himself at the height where it maintains the intelligence of an independent man who exists only for himself. Let us confess: For a long time, for a very long time, the world has not seen such an independent man regarding the power that he exercises and that redirects him towards a good that is other than his own — the only way to assure his total personal independence. "I am, in the realm of the possible, a free man."

This is because power is voracious. It enslaves its possessor. "I am the biggest slave among men," moaned Napoleon. This is illustrated in a shockingly degrading way with the dreadful spectacle of contemporary lovers of power and all those who aspire to stick to power in the hope of being taken for it. Whoever wants power for power's sake radically loses his independence. All of his acts are determined by power and not by his governing liberty. He debases himself to the level of erotic maniacs whom Venus, at the crossroads of this, mercilessly chains up.

The people know all of that instinctively. They know that power must be independent in order to be exercised. They are unfamiliar with the principle of noncontradiction and its logical formula, but they can guess that a dependent power is more impossible than a square circle. The people know this so well that, at the first demagogic excitement, they give themselves to the first leader who comes on the scene. One could say that he is the master of all his tones and that all power springs from his decisions, but he knows that he is nothing. As Simone Weil writes, "Humans are starving to obey." Obedience is such a vital need of the people that they are ready to give themselves to anyone. The people know that they cannot live without being commanded, without having an independent power above them.

The art of the sophists and demagogues is to turn this instructive tendency of the people towards themselves, by persuading the people that submitting to the power of others is beneath them. This impure power that they acquire is no less a power if they exercise it. It is no less independent because all power is independent. Leaders need only continual flattery to keep it in their possession. Rebellion is not a state of the popular soul except in cases of extreme and intolerable injustice. The permanent revolution that smoulders today in the conscience and even the unconscious of the people was introduced from outside, like a foreign body that makes them suffer and go delirious through rivalries that arise between lovers of power.

Contrary to all received ideas, it is not revolution that engenders democracy, but it is democracy and its large factions that engender revolution. We can write all the constitutions that we want that attribute power to the people. It will only ever be an atrocious trickery. An unchanging psychology opposes it. The people's obedience to a power that is independent of them is an unshakable axis. Contemporary "intellectuals"—those whom Bernanos[5] furiously held for imbeciles until they could provide proof to the contrary—are capable of dreaming forever of the people's power. As soon as their dreams are made concrete in facts and are submitted to the test of reality, those dreams will obey the principle of contradiction that drives power to exclude dependence.

Power's independence risks making it dangerous if it is not tamed by whoever exercises it. Its tendency is to grow without limits. We see this

5   Georges Bernanos (1888–1948), French author who is perhaps best known in English for his book, *Diary of a Country Priest*.

in all the countries where statism is rampant. Statism's characteristic, that is, socialism, is to be incapable of checking the extension of power because it lacks a human face. An anonymous power that is held by a party, religion, or race has no limits. Only the man who holds power can put the brakes on power because he alone is bestowed with self-mastery. Tyranny is at its height when the power-holder confuses himself with the mass of the people in order to mask his game. Power expands endlessly without being stopped by the man who is constantly occupied with maneuvering the people or by the congenitally powerless people. Recent history proves this eloquently. The absolute monarchs of the past are pygmies when we consider the gigantic development of contemporary democratic and totalitarian socialism in all its forms. Salazar has the unheard of merit of not ever following this slope: "I never flattered men or the masses, in front of whom so many bow down today in an attitude of hypocritical or abject servility."

The peoples of the world know this through tragic and terrible experience. For two centuries, they have gone from deception to deception. An immense and deaf aspiration grows in them for an independent power which would be held by an independent man who can moderate the exercise of power in adapting it to its appropriate end, which is the national interest. Only degenerate peoples, destined for death, do not feel this sentiment. In a country as corrupted by pseudo-democracy as France, Mr. Pinay's[6] success is the sign of this, despite political maneuvers to block it. It is the same in Spain with General Franco, in Germany with Chancellor Adenauer, and in Belgium where the dynasty has been maintained despite ten years of systematic defamation orchestrated by the pseudo-democrats.

It is impossible for a people not to admire a statesman who has vanquished and domesticated the demon of power. The cult that our ancestors devoted to their kings proves this. If the monarchs of the past were venerated at nearly all times by their people, if the monarchical system lasted so long in Europe, it is insofar as the hereditary transmission of power that is the heart of monarchy possesses a limit to power. Whoever transmits a heritage to his descendants is concerned not only that it be the least onerous possible. He also incites his successors to moderation. Historical experience incontestably proves that hereditary power is more moderate than a new and burning power over which men tend to become intoxicated. Experience proves that recently-acquired power is heavier to sustain than a continuous power that is submitted to the law of time and usage.

Now that the monarchies are disappearing, the entire problem of power and its moderation

6    Antoine Pinay (1891–1994) was a French politician briefly Prime Minister from 1952 to 1953.

must be taken on again. It is a matter of knowing how the new power that succeeds monarchies can be measured and made proportionate to the people who come under its influence. In other words, it is a matter of knowing how power becomes human, in spite of the actual propensity of power to become inhumane.

Salazar brings us this solution through his person. It is evident that today power cannot develop into tyranny or anarchy, which then leads to a harsher tyranny, without a perpetual sacrifice of self on the part of the individual exercising that power. That which a short while ago was done without much effort by a monarch thanks to the oil of an uncontested tradition poured into the political and social machine can no longer be accomplished without an exceptional mastery of self and a rigorous stoicism. In the past, institutions comforted people. The institution of marriage propped up shaky marriages. Today, it is faithful spouses who carry on their frail shoulders the destiny of this institution menaced by universal folly. Whereas in the past the state sustained those who governed it through its underlying stability, now it is the moral force of the heads of state who have to sustain and consolidate the state itself.

Thus Salazar.

Here is a man who, as master of the state, gives it his whole life rather than demanding everything from it. His refusal of all of the personal advantages that power never fails to grant to those who possess it is unparalleled. Salazar's austerity is legendary in Portugal. Salazar carried power like a "cross." This is the exact image: it is necessary that a statesman bear power like a salvific "cross." Salazar renounced having a family. He was horrified by spectacular exhibitions, flamboyant discourses, and titles and public honors. He only made enough to live modestly. He continued to live from his professor's salary. He lived in a small house. Salazar is alone before himself and before God. Every day, he hoped to terminate this load that he had not sought and that did not conform to his desires. He exercised power without desiring it in the way that today's politicians desire it. He exercised power without being carried aloft by the function like the kings of yesteryear. Nothing — neither his character nor his profession — prepared him for the task which he unwaveringly assumed for twenty-five years. Nothing prepared him aside from a complete detachment to himself and a total indifference to what other men passionately sought.

Today there is no other way to regenerate power, to restore the state, and to save the nation.

It is through the power he had over himself that Salazar was able to tame power when it was offered to him. A free and independent man, he was not the slave to this power which intoxicates so many strong men and weakens so many feeble men. Outside of himself, having mastered his own master, Salazar handled power as something that unites in no way with his being nor invades his ego. He could therefore master power and bend it to the proposed objective that he was undeniably pursuing: the good of his people and, over everything, peace — this peace that the old theologians called "the tranquility of order." The inhumanity he exercised towards himself won humanity for others. With an insignia of nobility, the humble laborer's son sacrificed everything for Portugal like his ancestors sowing the fields. In the desert of contemporary politics which is ravaged by democratic locusts and great totalitarian predators, here the very simple figure of a man rose. One can hardly distinguish the rising sands at the ends of the Earth and his tireless work.

Today, to be superior to the power that one possesses is almost miraculous — it is a sort of "divine grace," a *theia moira*, which Plato would have made the theme of a dialogue if he had known.

# Reflections from the Margins of the National Portuguese Revolution

PIERRE GAXOTTE

O NE OF THE GREAT EVILS OF our time is the degrading and debasing of politics in so many areas. In some places, this is an apocalyptic manifestation of an imposed force and a lie, in other places a clamor of inconsistent promises and unimpeded demands, an endless and systematic discussion of things that cannot be discussed, an outburst of passions, and a sterile agitation that repulses the man of science and the innovator.

Politics is a science, the science of the public good. Parties are not free to decide about this. The imagination also does not have the liberty to build any kind of kingdom. Certainly, every day the statesman must apply moderation, a judicious choice of moment and means, a certain publicity that is capable of creating or maintaining a collective state of conscience, and the setting up of a public force which is powerful enough to impose respect for power and to protect the unity of the country. Politics remains no less a science, of course not mathematical, but nevertheless capable of certitude, discipline, and an order which does not do well with capriciously planted traps of deceitful skepticism.

This serious, scientific, and eternal politics is the only one that can provoke the rallying of intelligences by dispersing the atmosphere of anxiety, discouragement, doubt, and passive acceptance that pushes so many free spirits towards total abdication at the profit of communist solutions. Every civilized man is grateful to Mr. Salazar for having given to politics his great dignity and for having affirmed in good time the great certitudes on which the political edifice can be built. Thanks to Salazar, in the middle of the worst war ever Portugal could mend the damage of the past in peace without involuntarily being dragged into something according to the dictates of imitation, fashion, and appeals.

Healthy politics is subordinate to the interest of the most real, vast, and resistant community. In the past, that community was Christendom, but the Reformation fractured it. Today, it is the nation. The word *real* excludes humanity, which has never existed in itself. We do not know if it will ever exist because it is more divided now than it was in the time of the Roman Empire. The word *resistant* excludes confederations, coalitions, and alliances that, while useful and even necessary at times, do not denote these superior realities of which we speak. The three adjectives used together — real, vast, and resistant — condemn the uniformizing of structures that were implanted in many European countries by English parliamentary institutions. These institutions are the British product *par excellence*, born from British history and directly derived from Anglo-Norman feudalism. It therefore goes without saying that, to discover the correct route, Mr. Salazar had to "dive into the abundant source of Portuguese institutions" in order to extract "usable elements" from the national tradition. The expression is from the President himself (speech on 11/22/51). This must be emphasized because tradition is not the transmission of just anything; it is the transmission of the beautiful and the true.

A foreigner would be badly positioned to describe and judge the work that has been accomplished. But he could derive at least a few lessons. Firstly, the head of a people, the head of a government, has an invaluable advantage when he is able to lean on political thinking, on a doctrine founded in reason and verified by history and experience. A head of government would be continually tempted by others if he were merely skillful, opportunistic, and full of know-how. Couldn't what succeeded elsewhere succeed in his country? Wouldn't he therefore be going against the genius of the nation, of its needs, and of geography itself? We can arbitrarily simplify things even more. Most often, the world offers only a confused spectacle, a free-for-all of rival systems that each have their victories and successes. Will each be tried one after the other? It is still necessary to be careful about confusing inviolable sacred principles and subordinate techniques with output that must be constantly measured.

In 1936 in Braga Mr. Salazar said, "We will not discuss God and virtue; we will not discuss the Fatherland and its history; we will not discuss the family and its moral code; we will not discuss honor and the duty of work." From this declaration, one can see the logical consequences going from respect for the human person to the transmission of cultural patrimonies. But what would the result be in the economic domain? Liberalism or a directed economy? In truth, this is an argument over words. Liberalism and a directed economy are no longer at odds because even if liberalism or, more precisely, the market economy, made a triumphant demonstration of its benefits in Germany, this liberalism has almost nothing in common with the liberalism of theoreticians. It allows for workers unions and repeated government interventions. Everything is a matter of moderation, surveillance, and wisdom. Moderation is not lacking in Portugal. The most ordinary function of the government is precisely a function of choice and synthesis. Judicious corporatism is synthesis. It is the same for all of the liberties.

The real exercise of political liberties depends not on constitutional formulas, but on the moral state of the country, its level of civic education, its patriotism, its respect for justice, its habits of tolerance, and its peaceful or violent customs. An act can be excellent and offend liberty. An act can proceed from the liberty that is the most formally written in laws and lead a people to death. Nothing can be condemned, nothing can be approved in the name of liberty alone. Liberty is not at the beginning, but at the end. It is not at the root, but at the blossoming of human virtue. Improving a people is preparing them for more freedom.

The French monarchy was called "absolute" because it was without mixture. No political principle altered or balanced the royal principle. That does not signify that it was tyrannical. All the old legalists carefully drew the distinction. Monarchy found its limits in itself in the respect for the fundamental laws that it subsumed — in sum, all the acquired rights, all the contracts made with the sovereign, and all the precedents which were susceptible to bringing consequences. It is also with pride that a French person finds in a very important discourse of Mr. Salazar (*My Testimony*, 1-7-49) a theory that proceeds from the most distant point of France's national history: "Power needs to feel limited, to act within limits. It needs internal limits that derive from the consciences of the governed themselves, the existence of laws and regular functioning of other organs of sovereignty, and external limits that are made up of the public judgment which is an opinion that will be enlightened and devoid of passion." No French person can forget that on the first page of *A Peaceful Revolution*, Mr. Salazar wrote: "I am most indebted to the French."

If Portugal's phenomenal recovery was possible and it was able to remain totally peaceful in the middle of convulsions that shook the world, it is undoubtedly necessary to hold up high the merit and glory to the men who guided it through danger, in particular to Marshal Carmona[1] and General Craveiro Lopes[2], Presidents of the Republic, and to the Professor Oliveira Salazar, President of the Council. But their efforts would have been in vain if they had not had authority and continuity at the same time. It was in May, 1926 that the army triggered the movement that, with the consent of the entire country, constituted the point of departure for the National Revolution. The first budget established by Mr. Salazar was that of 1928-29. While Portugal had lived in an endemic revolutionary state since the Republic's establishment in 1910, for more than a quarter of a century, it lived in a state of absolute political stability.

---

1   António Óscar Fragoso Carmona (1869–1951) served as Prime Minister of Portugal from 1926 to 1928 and the 11th President from 1926 until 1951.
2   Francisco Higino Craveiro Lopes (1894–1964) was the 12th President of Portugal having succeeded Carmona.

Without continuity, there is no serious work. Without continuity, there is no constructive work or order. Without continuity, there is no plan or progress. In truth, it is an extraordinary thing to be able to associate the idea of progress and the spirit of revolution in good faith. Science advances step by step by tying the work of today with that of the past, the work of the current generation with discoveries of previous generations. In contrast, true revolutionaries, taking the opposite approach, strive to demolish cumbersome structures in order to build from new. This is not a matter of denying the explosive force of the revolutionary idea, but to show the internal contradiction and, by weighing everything, the irreparable frivolity. Now, at its deepest level, the people are serious. Life is serious. It is a serious thing to earn a salary, to work, to use a tool, to raise children, and to fight against sickness, challenges, and suffering.

Projects that bring happiness and abundance merely through official means are not serious. It is also not serious to believe that a nation that is sick, tired, and shaken by troubles and insecurity can miraculously be cured by a rapid operation or by a sudden return of confidence. Great political triumphs come from a succession of acts, from time, and from patience. History teaches this. How many vast empires, hastily founded in victory, crumbled down in a single day, at the first defeat? A homeland is not born from

a contract that is signed one beautiful morning.
It is made slowly. It is not conserved in anarchy
and improvisation.

Mr. Salazar stated on December 9, 1934,

> Concentration cannot guarantee useful
> results if the effort is not continuous:
> To finish what one starts and not to
> start something without being sure of
> bringing things to the end. Continuity
> can be considered as a type of concen-
> tration in time and space because it
> demands the inclusion of problems or
> their parts in a system or plan that is
> to be executed according to the most
> rational order from the political, tech-
> nical, or economic point of view. There
> is nothing more contrary to the habits
> of a disordered or simply direction-
> less administration than the spirit
> of method. Nothing is more difficult
> than to have long-term action plans
> adopted which do not lend them-
> selves to improvisation, momentary
> fantasies and desires, the satisfaction
> of the best-supported interests, and
> private initiatives of agents, all of
> which are so appreciated and subject
> to acknowledgment. But there is also
> no better use of public funds and no
> more efficient defense of the equality

of everyone than this methodical principle applied to national problems.

What can be added to that?

The problem of continuity, however, comes
from those who have not ceased to preoccupy
Mr. Salazar. The future of a given accomplishment
depends on the solution that is to be found and
adopted. Mr. Salazar has addressed the problem
of the monarchy several times. A French monar-
chist cannot remain cold to what he said:

> When it comes to long-term politics,
> in other words an idea of government
> that is projected into the future and
> that has to be accomplished over many
> years, one has to recognize that mon-
> archies possess in their power superior
> means than republics do. (11/22/51)

No one can doubt this. As regards the conditions of the Portuguese nation, it is not the
task of a foreigner to address it. In his October
20, 1949 discourse to the National Assembly,
Mr. Salazar expressed himself with infinite dignity and candor. Let us retain only this phrase,
which perhaps summarizes the whole thing: "The
country has no interest in having a monarchy for
three months, nor three years."

Please pardon these disjointed reflections. I
wrote them in the margins of brochures and mag-
azines, and recopied them, without much order

nor with the vanity of novelty. If it is true, as Mr. Maurras wrote, that the common character of every civilization consists in a sole fact, which is to say that the individual who comes into the world in a "civilization" finds incomparably more than he brings to it, one can say that for a quarter of a century, the "civilizational" capital held by Portugal has prodigiously increased.

# Salazar the Wise Man

## GUSTAVE THIBON

PRESIDENT SALAZAR HAS THE well-established reputation of being a taciturn man. When he decides to speak, it is to truly say something. His words are then the fruit of meditation and experience, and they possess the weight of silence.

Such an example makes me circumspect. The man who, for a quarter of a century and in the most difficult circumstances in history, knew how to incarnate the destiny of the noble Portuguese nation only had to make prefabricated, all-purpose praises. An homage, to not be out of place, must have the bareness and the rigor of a testimony.

I know the works of Salazar and I have seen the man. And of all the terms that come to my spirit when I think of him, "wise man" spontaneously takes first place. A wise man is not only a theoretician or a technician. He is a man who, according to the admirable word of Plato, opens himself to the truth of all of his soul, for whom ideas are a food of the interior life and a principle of action, and of which the spirit, nourished by the complementary juices of reflection and experience, place themselves for all intents and purposes at the confluence of the ideal and the real. All that is needed to be a valid theoretician or technician is a well-organized brain, but the wise man needs to be a complete man.

Salazar is a man and — rare and precious thing among those marked with a brilliant destiny — he remained a man. One of the most cruel things that the experience of humanity has taught me is the harmful and dehumanizing influence on those who are the elected — or rather victims — of power and glory. As the popular expression goes: "They no longer knew themselves." They confused the character with the person, and social elevation with interior grandeur. It is like a poisoning in which the great symptoms are the swelling of the ego and the atrophy of the soul.

Nothing of this was found in Salazar. One does not crash into his ego, but, across the veil of modesty with which he covers his feelings, one can often distinguish his soul. Moreover, power for him is not a poison but a heavy load. I have rarely met someone who, precisely because he remained himself, was so scarcely "full of himself." The first principle of Socratic wisdom (*nosce teipsum*) permeates the inner life of this silent and contemplative man. For proof, it is enough to see with the keen lucidity, affability, detachment, and occasionally ironic discretion with which he speaks of his own self and justifies his work in front of his adversaries. One could write an admirable chapter on psychology: "Salazar, witness and judge of himself." He is legitimately proud of the work that has been done, but he modestly confesses to imperfections, and he carefully avoids above all to fall into the criminal error of dictators who, believing themselves to be necessary, so easily forget that they are not eternal.

The passion that surrounds him warms and encourages him, but does not intoxicate him. This is to the point where he himself reacts against the myth of the unique and infallible leader:

> I am undoubtedly aware of the support I have. But I have to recall that I always fought — even against the dominant tendency of the moment — so that we would not have to cede to the temptation to incarnate in one man the future of a work that, in its extent, eclipses him. I am only one ring that does not want to let itself be twisted or broken — a simple ring in a chain that unites with another in the service to the Nation.

On another occasion, he said: "We Portuguese, we all have around the same stature."

He is also aware of the terrible danger from the moral anesthesia that the habit of power weighs on leaders. Far from seeing himself as infallible, he confesses his limits and expresses his scruples: "My only regret is not having learned more in order to be wrong less often," he declared at the University of Coimbra. And in a speech to the army:

> In general, the habit of power dulls one's sensitivity a little. The journey already taken makes the point of departure more distant and blurry. Contact with rivalries, interests, and human weaknesses removes certain hopes and fills the spirit with disillusion when it does not discourage. That happens to strong men with lots of experience as a result of the wear from life. No one can be certain of never failing or giving up. There are moments, when listening to legitimately strong criticism about facts that reveal deficiencies that need addressing or abuse that needs to be suppressed or punished, when I ask myself if I hadn't already conformed to similar distractions, errors, or abuse in considering them as inevitable and uncontrollable.

These beautiful words produce a sound that does not deceive. The Emperor Marcus Aurelius gave himself the rule of life, "to go from one affair of state to another without losing the view of God in the interior." Without wanting to encroach on a secret that does not belong to humans, I believe that we can apply the same formula to Salazar, the silent and solitary one. Everything, in his private and public life, reveals a man who, despite all the internal and external obstacles, knew how to conserve his virgin and awakened soul and preserve it from two great dangers that drive the exercise of power: prideful corruption and the sclerosis of habit.

This wisdom, founded on clear self-knowledge, expanded with Salazar into a clear vision of things. It is at the basis of a very special political realism for which we can undoubtedly find certain antecedents in history but that, by its weighing, finesse of equilibrium, and, above all, animating spirit, distinguishes itself from everything that precedes it.

Roughly speaking, politicians can be divided into two large categories: theoreticians and technicians or, if you like, idealists and materialists. The former consider humans to be pure spirit while the latter deem humans to be vulgar mechanisms of interests and passions. Today, the pseudo-prophets of decadent democracies and the leaders of Marxist dictatorships represent these two opposing tendencies — but they hypocritically mix one with the other in concrete life. Everyone knows, for example, the sordid interests that hide behind demagogic idealism and the resounding appeals to ideals and heroism that the apostles of dialectical materialism issue every day.

But — this is one very significant thing that has not been adequately noted — the theoreticians and technicians of politics, so opposed as their principles may be, meet on a common basis: belief in humanity's unlimited progress and the naive conviction that simple reform of institutions will suffice in eliminating social imperfections and evil, which is to say, suffice in changing human nature itself. The idealism of 1789 and the Marxist materialism of our era perfectly concord on this point. Such misguided optimism can be very well explained, moreover, by the conception of humans that is the point of departure for these utopias.

Down here there are two things that are extremely easy to handle and with which all combinations and transformations are possible: disembodied thought (the spirit is swift) and inanimate matter (testified to by fantastic technological progress). If therefore we reduce humans to one of these two things, no hope, even the most senseless, is prohibited, and the strangest pipe dreams can become reality.

Unfortunately, these ideologues, filled with the worst spirit of abstraction, forget that at the confluence of an overly-swift spirit and overly-docile matter, too materialist to follow the spirit in its flight and too spiritual for marrying servility with matter, there is a man with a mysterious composition of each of these. This man — the real man who predates all the divisions of abstraction — is the object of political science. It is on him that Salazar's wisdom leans.

He says, "In this world where everything changes, that which changes the least is man himself. This is the first principle of sound politics: To not want at any price to adapt man to the changes that shake the world, but to try to adapt these changes to man's external nature."

Attentive to the whole person, Salazar's politics is neither idealist nor materialist. It is realist in the vastest and highest sense of the word. Salazar believes in the ideal, in liberty, love — in all the spiritual values — but, convinced like Richelieu that the nations, unlike individuals, find their salvation uniquely in this world, he keeps watch over the effective embodiment of these values more than over their verbal proclamation. This is so because in politics results count more than intentions, and the leader must know how to calculate the ideal amount of resources that can sustain the real and the amount of liberty compatible with the safeguard of authority and the maintenance of order. In this domain, the most beautiful success is still poorly hewn between the complementary demands in law and opposition from the real world of fact. It is the ransom of human infirmity that weighs the most heavily on the life of cities and on that of individuals.

Chateaubriand said,[1] "We must not shake the columns of the Temple. We can build the future on it." If I had to condense Salazar's social and political attitude into a formula, I would say: conservation for renewal. Save the past, not as a museum artifact or a funerary monument, but as the living mold of the future.

Salazar was reproached for being a pessimist when confronted with the great movements of ideas and attitudes that, today, are accelerating and modifying the course of history. We have seen why he cannot be optimistic in the manner of those who treat man like an angel or a machine. What people call his pessimism, I rather call prudence, mental clarity, and the sense of the possible. He does not refuse change. He does not pretend that the evolution of his country stopped with him and his work. He only fears to release the prey for the shadow and fears paying too much for the transformations which have undemonstrated value: "Humanity always finishes by finding its way. That is not the problem. The problem is that humanity discovers the distinct situation of immeasurable and unrivaled

---

1    François-René de Chateaubriand (1768–1848) was a French writer, politician, and historian whose work, *The Genius of Christianity*, Christopher Blum notes, was "epoch-making" and "the pivot between the classicism of the eighteenth century and the romanticism of the nineteenth." (*Critics of the Enlightenment*, Wilmington: DE, ISI, 2004), intro. xx

ruin and suffering as the unreasonably high price
of certain historical turns."

To avoid this overly-certain inconvenience of
still-problematic goods, the future must be con-
nected to the past and must not introduce into
the frame of history solutions of continuity that
negate life. "The evil that one does is heavier than
the good that one dreams of," the old democrat
Victor Hugo said, in a flash of good sense, to
impatient revolutionaries who saw renewal as
meaning destruction above all. Salazar responded
in a similar way to some of his political adversaries who dared declare their intent, in the electoral
campaign of 1949, to destroy whatever exists and
to see afterwards about the remainder: "Frighten-
ing words to hear: destroy, the remainder.... But
the remainder is everything: life, health, the work
of the Portuguese. It's the security of families and
home; it's the country's progress ... it's the aspiration to culture and well-being. It's public order
and justice in social relations. The remainder?
But the remainder is the interests, the problems,
and the life of the nation, its soul, its type of
civilization and culture, its history and radiance
in the world ... its prestige, its dignity ..."

Like his peasant forefathers, Salazar, a reformer
of institutions, respects the slowness and continuity of life (*natura non facit saltus...*). He does
not purport, in the fashion of a creator and
all-powerful God, to start from zero or to plant
seeds in the void. He patiently tries to graft what

is needed onto what is already there. To launch
his action, it is not enough that a certain reform
seems desirable to him. First of all, he works to
make it possible. And his wisdom does not over-
look that this margin of possibilities, more or less
vast according to the state of people's spirits and
the historical conjuncture, is never unlimited.
"Politics is a domain in which the absolute, which
is to say, the unlimited, is excluded everywhere."
Those who deny the limits of human power
and want to achieve the absolute only succeed
at destroying the relative. Holderlin's[2] words,
"society becomes a hell to the extent that one
wants to make it into a paradise," have received
the most shockingly harmful confirmations since
the era in which they were pronounced. Salazar
does not want to make Portugal into a paradise.
His ambition is to make livable the part of the
Earth over which destiny granted him authority.

He never paid with false money, and all forms
of inflation horrify him — commencing with
verbal inflation. He knows only too well what
hides behind the "curtain of smoke" deployed by
certain revolutionary intellectuals and to what
extent. In this he follows Scripture which says
that the lie sweetest to the mouth is bitter to
the guts. Hollow promises, fanciful plans, the
appeal to the most troubled passions — the entire

2   Friedrich Hölderlin (1770–1843) was a German poet
and philosopher and an influential figure in the German
Romantic movement.

arsenals of street performers and illusionists of demagoguery return to the abyss when they come into contact with him. He only needs two words to get rid of the corruptors of the people whose tactic, he says, "consists of denying the evidence and demanding the impossible."

Confronted with his adversaries, Salazar refutes dreams with reality and words with fact. It does not matter to him very much when a human or social value is proclaimed in sonorous words or hidden in a legislative text. What interests him is how it manifests itself in attitudes. To those who, just after the end of the Second World War reproached him, in the victorious euphoria of "democratic" ideas, for having restricted the liberties of the Portuguese people, he responded with this admirable lesson of true political realism: "The experience that we have acquired has taught us that in public liberties, if there is any interest in knowing to what extent they are recognized, their effective guarantee matters even more. Suffice it to say that these liberties are only of interest as long as they can be exercised and not when they are promulgated... If we consider this problem in the light of today, its true time, we arrive at two conclusions: first, if we set the facts in order, in Portugal today we have more liberty than ever before; second, with regard to principles, the degree of genuine public liberties depends on the capacity of the citizens, and not on a magnanimous concession of the state."

"You will know them by their fruits": This evangelical truth applies perhaps even more strongly to political regimes (of which the fruits are visible and are harvested here below) than to individuals whose secret intentions will only become visible in eternal life. It suffices to weigh the balance of two quarters of a century of Portuguese history, that which is dominated by the figure of Salazar, with that which preceded him, to distinguish the field full of the grain of real things from the field full of straw words. Salazar thinks less of defining and proclaiming the liberties of the Portuguese people than of leading this people to the degree of maturity that provides for the fruitful and non-perilous exercise of that liberty. The demagogues who exalt liberty without cultivating the human terrain where this liberty germinates resemble someone who, wanting to instruct an ignorant person, gives him a library as a present without thinking of first teaching him to read.

This very real concern for the real man is at the center of Salazar's politics and gives him a unique place among statesmen. He is preoccupied above all with the values of spirit and soul, and the spontaneous social foundation that the state authority can either aid or thwart but never supplement. What causes him anxiety is the decline of these same eternal values: this erosion of human nature and this crumbling of customs and traditions that transform individuals into anonymous and interchangeable atoms. No one is more hostile to the myth of the totalitarian state than this so-called dictator. He only conceives of the state as an instrument to save man and help him flourish. Institutions and laws only interest him as guardians of customs and souls. It is not he who confused the river and the dam, or the plant and the stake!

Yet, some object, Salazar exercises a rigorous authority over his country, and the Portuguese state is a strong state that very closely controls the nation's diverse activities. No doubt, but this is for the sake of remedy or provision rather than food itself. The bolstering of state authority as operated by Salazar does not correspond to his political ideal, but to harsh necessities imposed by the misfortune of the time. It is a fact of experience that actual men, wrenched from their natural environments, depend, in equal measure, on superstructures that are inspired or imposed by the central power: The more fragile a plant's roots are, the more it needs a stake. Salazar notes, "The constitution of the family, religious organization, private economy, spontaneous and voluntary association for cultural, moral, and athletic ends … this all seems to oscillate according to the salutary or evil impetus of power and effectively depends on it." It is the paradox of our epoch that the central power has an unending need to revive and control social organisms that, normally, would serve as a counterweight and a brake. It is certainly not a good that we should rejoice over, but it is a fact that we need to take into consideration.

Even more: if the modern state must be strong in order to support the positive aspirations of man, it must equally be strong in order to neutralize or correct his negative tendencies. Our interior demons and the thousand harmful influences that agitate us from the outside can more easily prey on us than before because we lack roots. Salazar perfectly senses the novel obligation that this danger imposes on the state: "Immoderate desires, the mirage of happiness through wealth, the aspiration for the new and the unknown, the thirst for pleasure, the ambition for the inaccessible, the instability of ideas and sentiments — all of this characterizes a maladaptive epoque and leads to difficulties against which it is appropriate to be guarded." In the current confusion of ideas and sentiments, people's desires coincide less than ever with what they need. People nowadays often need to be saved despite themselves. The stake not only supplements the fragility of the roots, but also protects the tree against gusts of wind.

A strong dose of ignorance or bad faith is also needed to dare contest, in the name of a fanciful liberty, an authority as paternal as Salazar. Was Portugal really so free in the time of the Republic of 1911? Did it not know for fifteen years worse tyrannies that impede the good and unchain the bad: a rotten dictatorship of political parties and a bloody revolutionary dictatorship? And is it not pleasant now to see the wolves that have been deprived of their prey reproach the shepherd for abuse of power?

In his hierarchy of human types, Plato places in first place the politician, servant of the city, and in last place the demagogue or flatterer of the people. If the words "political" and "politician" have today taken on a pejorative sense, it is undoubtedly due to the fact that the majority of those who exercise or seek power incline towards the second type rather than towards the first.

Salazar, savior and guardian of a people, restores to politics its original purity. For twenty-five years, his life was nothing but an uninterrupted personal sacrifice to his work, and this work itself is in his spirit only a means that is ordered to a more profound end: the salvation of material and spiritual values that eclipse politics but still depend on it. The whole set of values constitute the soul of the nation, the milieu in which the souls of individuals bathe and develop until they emerge into eternity. At a time when, in so many countries, the chasm between political power and genuine national realities grows ever larger, the person and work of Salazar appears as an example and a call. In our perspective, we find in him one of the rare reasons not to despair of a world in which, at least in one country, power can still be exercised and conserved by a wise man.

# ABOUT THE CONTRIBUTORS

MARCEL DE CORTE (1905–1994) was a Belgian Thomistic philosopher and a contemporary of Jacques Maritain and Etienne Gilson. He taught at the University of Liège from 1932 until his retirement in 1975. He was one of the main contributors to the magazine, *Itinéraires*, founded by Jean Madiran. He was the author of over twenty books with a particular interest on social change at the heart of modernity. Some of his books include: *Philosophie des mœurs contemporaines* (1944), *Essai sur la fin d'une civilisation* (1949), *L'intelligence en péril de mort* (1969), and his books on the four cardinal virtues in the light of St. Thomas Aquinas (1973–1982). There is little of his work which has been translated into English.

PIERRE GAXOTTE (1895–1982) was a French historian and journalist who early on was a secretary for Charles Maurras. He would subsequently abandon his political activism and become a columnist for Le Figaro. His many historical works include: *La Révolution française* (1928), *La France de Louis XIV* (1946), and *Frédéric II, roi de Prusse* (1967). He was a member of *The French Academy.*

GUSTAVE THIBON (1903–2001), French Catholic philosopher, author of over twenty books and nominee for the Nobel Prize in Literature four times. Some of his works include: *Destin de l'Homme* (1941), *Diagnostics. Essai de Physiologie Sociale* in 1942 (translated into English as *What Ails Mankind?* by Sheed & Ward in 1947) as well as publishing Simone Weil's work *La Pesanteur et la Grâce* in 1947.

# ABOUT THE TRANSLATOR

BRIAN WELTER teaches advanced high school reading and writing. He is interested in French literature, medieval history and aesthetics. He has a BA in history and degrees in theology, including the DTh. He also has a graduate diploma in teaching English. In addition to French, he reads Italian, German, and Latin.

Lightning Source UK Ltd.
Milton Keynes UK
UKHW010640290721
387974UK00002B/432